THE STORY BEHIND
CINCO DE MAYO

JACK READER

PowerKiDS
press™

New York

Published in 2020 by The Rosen Publishing Group, Inc.
29 East 21st Street, New York, NY 10010

First Edition

Editor: Tanya Dellaccio
Book Design: Reann Nye

Photo Credits: Cover, p.1 Kobby Dagan; pp. 4, 6, 8, 10, 12, 14, 16, 18, 20, 22 (background) Preto Perola/Shutterstock.com; p. 5 Andrew Lichtenstein/Corbis News/Getty Images; p. 7 https://commons.wikimedia.org/wiki/File:Batalla_del_5_de_mayo_de_1862.jpg; p. 9 Sergio Mendoza Hochmann/Moment Unreleased/Getty Images; p. 11 Roberto Galan/Shutterstock.com; p. 13 https://commons.wikimedia.org/wiki/File:Vista_fuerte_derecha.JPG; p. 15 PAUL RATJE/AFP/Getty Images; p. 17 Scharfsinn/Shutterstock.com; p. 19 Kevork Djansezian/Getty Images; p. 21 Kit Leong/Shutterstock.com; p. 22 DOUGBERRY/E+/Getty Images.

Library of Congress Cataloging-in-Publication Data

Names: Reader, Jack, author.
Title: The story behind Cinco de Mayo / Jack Reader.
Description: New York : PowerKids Press, [2020] | Series: Holiday histories |
  Includes index.
Identifiers: LCCN 2018050205| ISBN 9781725300361 (pbk.) | ISBN 9781725300385
  (library bound) | ISBN 9781725300378 (6 pack)
Subjects: LCSH: Cinco de Mayo (Mexican holiday)-History-Juvenile
  literature. | Holidays-Mexico. | Holidays-United States. | Puebla,
  Battle of, Puebla de Zaragoza, Mexico, 1862-Juvenile literature. |
  Mexico-Social life and customs-Juvenile literature. | United
  States-Social life and customs-Juvenile literature.
Classification: LCC F1233 .R29 2020 | DDC 394.262-dc23
LC record available at https://lccn.loc.gov/2018050205

Manufactured in the United States of America

CPSIA Compliance Information: Batch #CSPK19. For Further Information contact Rosen Publishing, New York, New York at 1-800-237-9932.

CONTENTS

The Fifth of May

Cinco de Mayo is **celebrated** each year on May 5. Can you guess what "Cinco de Mayo" means? It's Spanish for "the fifth of May"! This holiday marks the date of a battle between France and Mexico in 1862. It celebrates Mexican **culture**.

Making Deals

In the mid-1800s, Mexico wasn't able to pay back money it owed to European countries. Britain, Spain, and France sent soldiers to Mexico to get the money they were owed. Britain and Spain made deals with Mexico, but French leaders decided to take over Mexican land.

The Battle of Puebla

On May 5, 1862, about 6,000 French troops **attacked** Puebla, a small city southeast of Mexico City. About 2,000 Mexican troops, led by General Ignacio Zaragoza, prepared for the attack. The Mexicans had fewer troops and supplies, and it wasn't likely they would win.

General Ignacio Zaragoza

The Battle of Puebla lasted the whole day. The French gave in after losing around 500 men, giving Mexico the **victory**. The Mexicans only lost about 100 fighters. The win brought great pride to the country, making May 5 a day of great importance.

Keeping History Alive

The city of Puebla was later renamed Puebla de Zaragoza, after the man who led the Mexican troops to victory. The battlefield was turned into a park, and one of the forts there was turned into a **museum**.

Fort Loreto Museum

13

Celebrating in Mexico

Cinco de Mayo has Mexican roots, but few places in Mexico outside of Puebla celebrate the holiday. In Puebla, there are speeches and parades for Cinco de Mayo. There's also tasty food, music, and dancing. People even act out the Battle of Puebla each year.

15

The United States

Cinco de Mayo is a popular holiday in the United States. It's celebrated throughout the country, more so in places where many Mexican Americans live. For some, the holiday is still all about Mexican culture. People celebrate with parades, different foods, dancing, and **mariachi music**.

mariachi band

In the 1960s, some Mexican Americans became part of the **civil rights movement**. This created interest in Mexican culture, and more people began celebrating Cinco de Mayo. Today, the biggest Cinco de Mayo celebration in the United States is in Los Angeles, California.

Holiday Mix-Up

Many people have forgotten the meaning behind Cinco de Mayo over the years. It's common in many places for the celebration to be just a day of partying. Some celebrations include hurtful **stereotypes** of Mexican culture.

Time to Celebrate

You can celebrate Cinco de Mayo on May 5, if you'd like. You can listen to mariachi music or learn a traditional Mexican dance. You can also enjoy a Mexican meal. Just remember the Battle of Puebla and the history behind this important day.

GLOSSARY

attack: To try to hurt, injure, or destroy something or someone, or the act of doing so.

celebrate: To do something special or enjoyable for an important event or holiday.

civil rights movement: A movement in the mid-1900s in the United States in which many people and groups worked for equality among all people.

culture: The beliefs and ways of life of a certain group of people.

mariachi music: A type of lively Mexican street music played by a band of trumpets and string instruments.

museum: A building in which interesting and valuable things are collected and shown to the public.

stereotype: An often unfair and untrue belief that some people have about all people or things with a particular trait or background.

victory: Success in defeating an enemy.

INDEX

WEBSITES

Due to the changing nature of Internet links, PowerKids Press has developed an online list of websites related to the subject of this book. This site is updated regularly. Please use this link to access the list: www.powerkidslinks.com/HH/cinco